# WISE SAYINGS

*of*

## ST

# PAUL

# WISE SAYINGS

*of*

## ST

# PAUL

LION

Compiled by Olivia Warburton
This edition copyright © 2011
Lion Hudson
The author asserts the moral right
to be identified as the author of
this work

A Lion Book
an imprint of
**Lion Hudson plc**
Wilkinson House, Jordan Hill Road,
Oxford OX2 8DR, England
www.lionhudson.com
ISBN 978 0 7459 5554 4

Distributed by:
UK: Marston Book Services, PO Box
269, Abingdon, Oxon, OX14 4YN
USA: Trafalgar Square Publishing, 814
N. Franklin Street, Chicago, IL 60610
USA Christian Market: Kregel
Publications, PO Box 2607, Grand
Rapids, MI 49501
First edition 2011
10 9 8 7 6 5 4 3 2 1 0
All rights reserved

**Acknowledgments**
pp. 14t, 18–19, 28–29, 32b, 42, 52–53:
Scripture quotations are from *The Holy
Bible, English Standard Version*, published
by HarperCollins Publishers, copyright
© 2001 Crossway Bibles, a division
of Good News Publishers. Used by
permission. All rights reserved.
pp. 11, 14b, 15b, 30t, 32t, 43: Scripture
quotations [marked GNB] are from
the *Good News Bible* published by the
Bible Societies and HarperCollins
Publishers, © American Bible Society
1994, used with permission. pp. 10,
12, 21, 24–25, 33, 36–37, 46–47,
57, 58–59: Scripture quotations taken
from the *Holy Bible, New International
Version*, copyright © 1973, 1978, 1984
International Bible Society. Used by
permission of Zondervan and Hodder &
Stoughton Limited. All rights reserved.
The 'NIV' and 'New International
Version' trademarks are registered in
the United States Patent and Trademark
Office by International Bible Society.
Use of either trademark requires the
permission of International Bible
Society. UK trademark number
1448790. pp. 31, 35, 44, 56t: *The New
King James Version* copyright © 1982,
1979 by Thomas Nelson, Inc. J.B.
Phillips Reprinted with the permission
of Simon & Schuster from *The New
Testament in Modern English*, Revised
Edition, translated by J. B. Phillips.
Copyright © 1958, 1960, 1972 by
J. B. Phillips. Reprinted from *The New
Testament in Modern English*, Revised
Edition, translated by J.B. Phillips.
Published by HarperCollins Publishers
Ltd. pp. 15t, 20, 22–23, 30b, 34, 48:
Scripture quotations are taken from
the *Holy Bible, New Living Translation*,
copyright © 1996. Used by permission
of Tyndale House Publishers, Inc.,
Wheaton, Illinois 60189. All rights
reserved. pp. 6, 13, 40, 45, 54–55,
56b: Scripture quotations are from the
*New Revised Standard Version* published
by HarperCollins Publishers, copyright
© 1989 by the Division of Christian
Education of the National Council of
the Churches of Christ in the USA,
and are used by permission. All rights
reserved.

A catalogue record for this book is
available from the British Library
Typeset in 10.5/12 Perpetua and 10/24
Zapfino
Printed and bound in China

ONTENTS

# INTRODUCTION

The apostle Paul stands in Christian history as a speaker, pastor, and theologian of unparalleled influence. His powerful exhortations and faithful encouragements transformed the early church — and have continued to inspire people ever since.

This book brings together some of his most incisive teachings, taken from his letters to the first churches. Despite the passing of 2,000 years, they are still as pertinent and applicable today as they were when first written.

*The fruit of the Spirit is love, joy, peace, patience, kindness, generosity, faithfulness, gentleness, and self-control.*

**GALATIANS 5:22–23**

# GOD'S POWER

The Son is the image of the invisible God, the firstborn over all creation. For in him all things were created: things in heaven and on earth, visible and invisible, whether thrones or powers or rulers or authorities; all things have been created through him and for him. He is before all things, and in him all things hold together.

COLOSSIANS 1:15–17

*All of us, then, reflect
the glory of the Lord with
uncovered faces; and that same
glory, coming from the Lord,
who is the Spirit, transforms
us into his likeness in an ever
greater degree of glory.*

**2 Corinthians 3:18**

So where does this leave the philosophers, the scholars, and the world's brilliant debaters? God has made the wisdom of this world look foolish. Since God in his wisdom saw to it that the world would never know him through human wisdom, he has used our foolish preaching to save those who believe. It is foolish to the Jews, who ask for signs from heaven. And it is foolish to the Greeks, who seek human wisdom. So when we preach that Christ was crucified, the Jews are offended and the Gentiles say it's all nonsense. But to those called by God to salvation, both Jews and Gentiles, Christ is the power of God and the wisdom of God. This foolish plan of God is wiser than the wisest of human plans, and God's weakness is stronger than the greatest of human strength.

1 CORINTHIANS 1:20–25

*If God is for us, who is against us?*
*He who did not withhold his own*
*Son, but gave him up for all of us,*
*will he not with him also give us*
*everything else?*

**ROMANS 8:31–32**

And we know that for those who
love God all things work together
for good, for those who are called
according to his purpose.

**ROMANS 8:28**

He who calls you will do it,
because he is faithful.

**1 THESSALONIANS 5:24**

I know how to live on almost nothing or with everything. I have learned the secret of living in every situation, whether it is with a full stomach or empty, with plenty or little. For I can do everything through Christ, who gives me strength.

**PHILIPPIANS 4:12–13**

May our Lord Jesus Christ himself and God our Father, who loved us and in his grace gave us unfailing courage and a firm hope, encourage you and strengthen you always to do and say what is good.

**2 THESSALONIANS 2:16–17**

# RELATIONSHIPS

So if there is any encouragement in Christ, any comfort from love, any participation in the Spirit, any affection and sympathy, complete my joy by being of the same mind, having the same love, being in full accord and of one mind. Do nothing from rivalry or conceit, but in humility count others more significant than yourselves. Let each of you look not only to his own interests, but also to the interests of others. Have this mind among yourselves, which is yours in Christ Jesus, who, though he was in the form of God, did not count equality with God a thing to be grasped, but made himself nothing, taking the form of a servant, being born in the likeness of men. And being found in human form, he humbled himself by becoming obedient to the point of death, even death on a cross.

Therefore God has highly exalted him and bestowed on him the name that is above every name, so that at the name of Jesus every knee should bow, in heaven and on earth and under the earth, and every tongue confess that Jesus Christ is Lord, to the glory of God the Father.

**PHILIPPIANS 2:1–11**

Because of the privilege and authority
God has given me, I give each of you this
warning: Don't think you are better than
you really are. Be honest in your evaluation
of yourselves, measuring yourselves by the
faith God has given us. Just as our bodies
have many parts and each part has a special
function, so it is with Christ's body. We are
many parts of one body, and we all
belong to each other.

**ROMANS 12:3–5**

Now if the foot should say, "Because I am not a hand, I do not belong to the body," it would not for that reason stop being part of the body. And if the ear should say, "Because I am not an eye, I do not belong to the body," it would not for that reason stop being part of the body. If the whole body were an eye, where would the sense of hearing be? If the whole body were an ear, where would the sense of smell be? But in fact God has placed the parts in the body, every one of them, just as he wanted them to be. If they were all one part, where would the body be? As it is, there are many parts, but one body.

**1 Corinthians 12:15—20**

Don't just pretend to love others. Really love them.

*Hate what is wrong.*

*Hold tightly to what is good.*

Love each other with genuine affection, and take
delight in honouring each other. Never be lazy,
but work hard and serve the Lord enthusiastically.
Rejoice in our confident hope. Be patient in trouble,
and keep on praying. When God's people are in need,
be ready to help them. Always be eager to
practice hospitality.

*live in*

Bless those who persecute you. Don't curse them;
pray that God will bless them. Be happy with those
who are happy, and weep with those who weep.
Live in harmony with each other. Don't be too proud
to enjoy the company of ordinary people.
And don't think you know it all!
Never pay back evil with more evil. Do things in such
a way that everyone can see you are honourable.
Do all that you can to live in peace with everyone.

**ROMANS 12:9–18**

*peace*

Now we ask you, brothers and sisters, to acknowledge those who work hard among you, who care for you in the Lord and who admonish you. Hold them in the highest regard in love because of their work. Live in peace with each other. And we urge you, brothers and sisters, warn those who are idle and disruptive, encourage the disheartened, help the weak, be patient with everyone.

Make sure that nobody pays back wrong for wrong, but always strive to do what is good for each other and for everyone else.

Rejoice always, pray continually, give thanks in all circumstances; for this is God's will for you in Christ Jesus.

**1 THESSALONIANS 5:12–18**

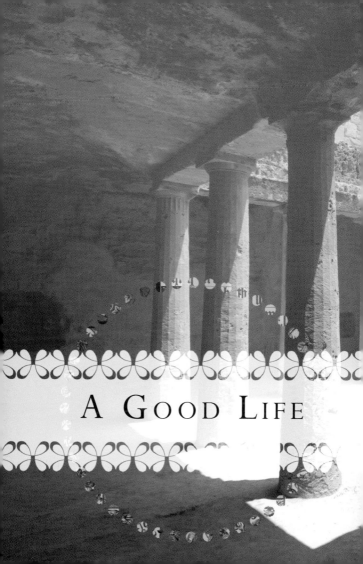

# A GOOD LIFE

For I know that nothing good dwells in me, that is, in my flesh. For I have the desire to do what is right, but not the ability to carry it out. For I do not do the good I want, but the evil I do not want is what I keep on doing. Now if I do what I do not want, it is no longer I who do it, but sin that dwells within me.

So I find it to be a law that when I want to do right, evil lies close at hand. For I delight in the law of God, in my inner being, but I see in my members another law waging war against the law of my mind and making me captive to the law of sin that dwells in my members. Wretched man that I am! Who will deliver me from this body of death? Thanks be to God through Jesus Christ our Lord!

**ROMANS 7:18–25**

"We are allowed to do anything," so they say. That is true, but not everything is good. "We are allowed to do anything" – but not everything is helpful. None of you should be looking to your own interests, but to the interests of others.

**1 Corinthians 10:23–24**

*For we are God's masterpiece. He has created us anew in Christ Jesus, so we can do the good things he planned for us long ago.*

**Ephesians 2:10**

But this I say: He who sows sparingly
will also reap sparingly, and he who sows
bountifully will also reap bountifully.
So let each one give as he purposes in his
heart, not grudgingly or of necessity;
for God loves a cheerful giver.
And God is able to make all grace
abound toward you, that you,
always having all sufficiency in all things,
may have an abundance for every good work.

**2 Corinthians 9:6–8**

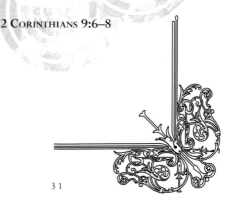

Make it your aim to live a quiet life, to mind your own business, and to earn your own living, just as we told you before. In this way you will win the respect of those who are not believers, and you will not have to depend on anyone for what you need.

**1 Thessalonians 4:11–12**

Do all things without grumbling or questioning, that you may be blameless and innocent, children of God without blemish in the midst of a crooked and twisted generation, among whom you shine as lights in the world, holding fast to the word of life.

**Philippians 2:14–16**

Do you not know that in a race all the runners run, but only one gets the prize? Run in such a way as to get the prize. Everyone who competes in the games goes into strict training. They do it to get a crown that will not last, but we do it to get a crown that will last forever.

**1 CORINTHIANS 9:24–25**

et true godliness with contentment is itself great wealth. After all, we brought nothing with us when we came into the world, and we can't take anything with us when we leave it. So if we have enough food and clothing, let us be content. But people who long to be rich fall into temptation and are trapped by many foolish and harmful desires that plunge them into ruin and destruction. For the love of money is the root of all kinds of evil. And some people, craving money, have wandered from the true faith and pierced themselves with many sorrows.

**1 TIMOTHY 6:6–10**

I beseech you therefore, brethren, by the mercies of God, that you present your bodies a living sacrifice, holy, acceptable to God, which is your reasonable service. And do not be conformed to this world, but be transformed by the renewing of your mind, that you may prove what is that good and acceptable and perfect will of God.

**ROMANS 12:1–2**

Rejoice in the Lord always. I will say it again: Rejoice! Let your gentleness be evident to all. The Lord is near. Do not be anxious about anything, but in every situation, by prayer and petition, with thanksgiving, present your requests to God. And the peace of God, which transcends all understanding, will guard your hearts and your minds in Christ Jesus.

Finally, brothers and sisters, whatever is true, whatever is noble, whatever is right, whatever is pure, whatever is lovely, whatever is admirable – if anything is excellent or praiseworthy – think about such things. Whatever you have learned or received or heard from me, or seen in me – put it into practice. And the God of peace will be with you.

**PHILIPPIANS 4:4–9**

*rejoice!*

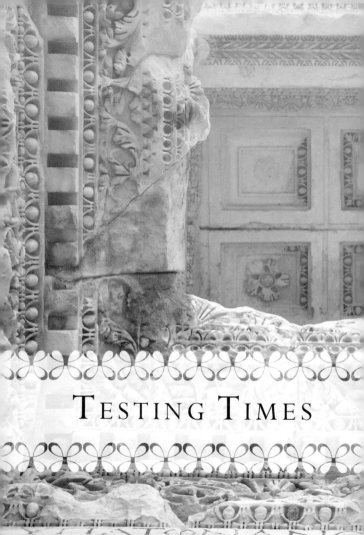

# TESTING TIMES

Yet whatever gains I had, these I have come to regard as loss because of Christ. More than that, I regard everything as loss because of the surpassing value of knowing Christ Jesus my Lord. For his sake I have suffered the loss of all things, and I regard them as rubbish, in order that I may gain Christ and be found in him, not having a righteousness of my own that comes from the law, but one that comes through faith in Christ, the righteousness from God based on faith. I want to know Christ and the power of his resurrection and the sharing of his sufferings by becoming like him in his death, if somehow I may attain the resurrection from the dead.

**Philippians 3:7–11**

found
in him

More than that, we rejoice in our sufferings, knowing that suffering produces endurance, and endurance produces character, and character produces hope, and hope does not put us to shame, because God's love has been poured into our hearts through the Holy Spirit who has been given to us.

**ROMANS 5:3–5**

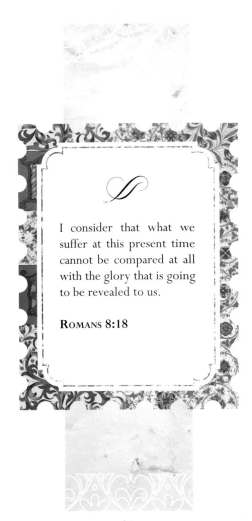

I consider that what we suffer at this present time cannot be compared at all with the glory that is going to be revealed to us.

**ROMANS 8:18**

Therefore let him who thinks he stands take heed lest he fall. No temptation has overtaken you except such as is common to man; but God is faithful, who will not allow you to be tempted beyond what you are able, but with the temptation will also make the way of escape, that you may be able to bear it.

1 CORINTHIANS 10:12–13

As for me, I am already being poured out as a libation, and the time of my departure has come. I have fought the good fight, I have finished the race, I have kept the faith. From now on there is reserved for me the crown of righteousness, which the Lord, the righteous judge, will give to me on that day, and not only to me but also to all who have longed for his appearing.

**2 Timothy 4:6–8**

But we have this treasure in jars of clay to show that this all-surpassing power is from God and not from us. We are hard pressed on every side, but not crushed; perplexed, but not in despair; persecuted, but not abandoned; struck down, but not destroyed. We always carry around in our body the death of Jesus, so that the life of Jesus may also be revealed in our body....

Therefore we do not lose heart.
Though outwardly we are wasting
away, yet inwardly we are being
renewed day by day. For our
light and momentary troubles are
achieving for us an eternal glory
that far outweighs them all. So we
fix our eyes not on what is seen,
but on what is unseen, since what
is seen is temporary, but what is
unseen is eternal.

2 Corinthians 4:7–10, 16–18

Be strong in the Lord and in his mighty power. Put on all of God's armour so that you will be able to stand firm against all strategies of the devil. For we are not fighting against flesh-and-blood enemies, but against evil rulers and authorities of the unseen world, against mighty powers in this dark world, and against evil spirits in the heavenly places.

Therefore, put on every piece of God's armour so you will be able to resist the enemy in the time of evil. Then after the battle you will still be standing firm. Stand your ground, putting on the belt of truth and the body armour of God's righteousness. For shoes, put on the peace that comes from the Good News so that you will be fully prepared. In addition to all of these, hold up the shield of faith to stop the fiery arrows of the devil. Put on salvation as your helmet, and take the sword of the Spirit, which is the word of God.

**EPHESIANS 6:10–17**

be strong

# GOD'S LOVE

Who shall separate us from the love of Christ? Shall tribulation, or distress, or persecution, or famine, or nakedness, or danger, or sword? As it is written,
"For your sake we are being killed all the day long; we are regarded as sheep to be slaughtered."

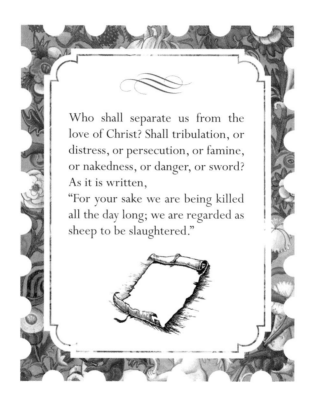

No, in all these things we are more than conquerors through him who loved us. For I am sure that neither death nor life, nor angels nor rulers, nor things present nor things to come, nor powers, nor height nor depth, nor anything else in all creation, will be able to separate us from the love of God in Christ Jesus our Lord.

**ROMANS 8:35—39**

As God's chosen ones, holy and beloved, clothe yourselves with compassion, kindness, humility, meekness, and patience. Bear with one another and, if anyone has a complaint against another, forgive each other; just as the Lord has forgiven you, so you also must forgive. Above all, clothe yourselves with love, which binds everything together in perfect harmony.

And let the peace of Christ rule
in your hearts, to which indeed
you were called in the one body.
And be thankful. Let the word
of Christ dwell in you richly;
teach and admonish one another
in all wisdom; and with gratitude
in your hearts sing psalms, hymns,
and spiritual songs to God.
And whatever you do, in word or
deed, do everything in the name of
the Lord Jesus, giving thanks to
God the Father through him.

COLOSSIANS 3:12–17

For while we were still weak, at the right time Christ died for the ungodly. Indeed, rarely will anyone die for a righteous person – though perhaps for a good person someone might actually dare to die. But God proves his love for us in that while we still were sinners Christ died for us.

ROMANS 5:6–8

When the kindness and the love of God our Saviour toward man appeared, not by works of righteousness which we have done, but according to His mercy He saved us, through the washing of regeneration and renewing of the Holy Spirit.

TITUS 3:4–5

And I pray that you, being rooted and established in love, may have power, together with all the Lord's holy people, to grasp how wide and long and high and deep is the love of Christ, and to know this love that surpasses knowledge – that you may be filled to the measure of all the fullness of God.

**EPHESIANS 3:17–19**

If I speak in the tongues of men and of angels, but have not love, I am only a resounding gong or a clanging cymbal. If I have the gift of prophecy and can fathom all mysteries and all knowledge, and if I have a faith that can move mountains, but have not love, I am nothing. If I give all I possess to the poor and surrender my body to the flames, but have not love, I gain nothing.

Love is patient, love is kind. It does not envy, it does not boast, it is not proud. It is not rude, it is not self-seeking, it is not easily angered, it keeps no record of wrongs. Love does not delight in evil but rejoices with the truth. It always protects, always trusts, always hopes, always perseveres.

Love never fails. But where there are prophecies, they will cease; where there are tongues, they will be stilled; where there is knowledge, it will pass away. For we know in part and we prophesy in part, but when perfection comes, the imperfect disappears. When I was a child, I talked like a child, I thought like a child, I reasoned like a child. When I became a man, I put childish ways behind me. Now we see but a poor reflection as in a mirror; then we shall see face to face. Now I know in part; then I shall know fully, even as I am fully known.

And now these three remain: faith, hope and love. But the greatest of these is love.

**1 CORINTHIANS 13:1–13**

# ACKNOWLEDGMENTS

BACKGROUNDS:
**iStock:** Jussi Santaniemi

ILLUMINATED MANUSCRIPTS:
**Alamy:** Classic Image
**Corbis:** Fine Art Photographic Library; The Gallery Collection

MOTIFS:
**iStock:** Ace_Create; Constance McGuire; Dave Smith; Gillian Mowbray; Jamie Farrant; Keith Bishop; Thezeus Sarris

PHOTOGRAPHS:
**Corbis:** pp. 6–7 Photolibrary; pp. 14–15 Renan Rosa/Aurora Photos; p. 18 Nico Tondini/Robert Harding World Imagery; pp. 26–27, 40–41, 49 Ocean; pp. 50–51 Aaron Horowitz
**iStock:** pp. 8–9 Aleksandar Nakic; pp. 16–17 Bryan Busovicki; p. 21 Chris Kocek; pp. 22–23 Grigorios Moraitis; pp. 36–37 Carole Gomez; pp. 38–39 Bojan Pavlukovic; pp. 46–47 PJ. Morley; pp. 54–55 Oleksandr Prykhodko; pp. 58–59 Max Homand

COVER
**Background:** Jussi Santoniemi/iStock
**Illuminated manuscript:** The Gallery Collection/Corbis
**Photograph:** Svenja-Foto/Corbis